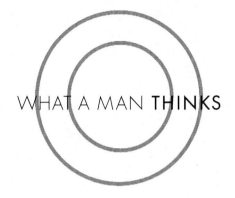

WHAT A MAN **THINKS**

WHAT A MAN **THINKS**

Understanding a man's heart
JAMES A. DUNKINS

Tate Publishing & Enterprises

Published by Tate Publishing & Enterprises, LLC
127 E. Trade Center Terrace | Mustang, Oklahoma 73064 USA
1.888.361.9473 | www.tatepublishing.com

Tate Publishing is committed to excellence in the publishing industry. The company reflects the philosophy established by the founders, based on Psalm 68:11,
"The Lord gave the word and great was the company of those who published it."

Book design copyright © 2008 by Tate Publishing, LLC. All rights reserved.
Cover design by Leah LeFlore
Interior design by Jonathan Lindsey

Published in the United States of America

ISBN: 978-1-60696-451-4
1. Poetry: General   2. Social Science: Men's Studies
08.10.29

DEDICATION

This book is dedicated to all of the hurting
and misunderstood men who need a voice.
Thank you for your honest and open
remarks about the real experiences
in your life.
This book is dedicated to you to encourage
you to be the man you were created to be.

CONTENTS

FOREWORD

Why a book of poems for men? I believe men are emotional creatures with no real outlet for their emotions. Therefore, most of our dysfunctional behavior is a result of a life out of balance. To be completely healthy, all men need to be in touch with their emotions, and they need people to understand.

This book will help you get your life in touch and in balance.

INTRODUCTION

This book consists of three dimensions of a man's life. It is comprised of the inner man, called *Me*, the surrendered man, called *God*, and the relational man, called *Us*.

Me

Me is designed to highlight some of the inward struggles of a man's heart that he is yearning to share but does not know how. It shows the contradictions and complications of his manhood as he comes to grips with his faults and failures while seeking a foundational truth to stand on. **Me** is a disguise for the cry for help that every man would like to utter but cannot sometimes because of pride, sometimes because of societal expectations, and his inability to communicate.

God

This is as close as you will ever see a man open up and talk about his innermost feelings. When men find God, they can surrender the direction and control of their life over into God's hands. The **God** section is filled with relief and surprise as a man finds a resting place for the demands and struggles of manhood. He learns that only through the eyes of God can he really see his true self and can admit his troubles.

Us

Us is focused on relationship issues from a man's perspective. The man feels that his roles are sometimes unfair, unmanageable, and unappreciated. He longs to understand what motivates his wife and his children so he can be the strength of the family. Any relationship is challenging to a man, married, unmarried, or looking to be married. It seems the longer a man is in a relationship, the less he understands. Sometimes he doesn't put in the energy that it takes to make the relationship work.

PART I

ME
"True wisdom only comes when a man is continually seeking to know himself better."

I'M A MAN

Don't talk to me like that.
Who you think you talking to?
You can't talk down to me.
I am running things or I am supposed to be.
So don't roll your eyes.
Don't you know I've got pride?
I'm a man.
Don't tell me I can't fix it and I need to throw that
away.
I will throw it away when I want to and
I will work on this thing all day.
I know I don't know what I am doing,
But that is not for you to say.
If it don't work, at least my head's still held high.
Don't you know I've got pride?
I'm a man.
You ain't gonna fix me anything to eat?
I just got off work; I know you did too.
But that is the kinda thing you are supposed to
do.
Yeah, I am going to sit right down on this couch.

But when I get up, you know I will be busier than you.

Why you worrying me? You don't tell me what to do.

I deserve to sit and relax a while.

Don't you know I've got pride?

I'm a man.

So what, I was late. At least I was there.

I don't know how long it takes to do your nails and hair.

I know you told me,

But you say a lot of things and usually I'm confused. I am getting mad.

You know it's your fault because you started this mess.

You should have left me alone when you first got in the car.

I really don't want to argue.

I can, but that is not my style.

Don't you know I've got pride?

I'm a man.

Just in case you're wondering,

I know I should say I'm sorry. I know I should apologize.

I know sometimes I treat you wrong, and I get all tangled up inside.

I should tell you that I love you, and you look good in that dress.

Sometimes I should take credit because you don't start all the mess.

The things I learn about being a man I know deep down inside are not true.

But even though I know it, I keep hurting you.

Sure wish I could forget about my pride.

I am a man, but I'm going to change.

IF I COULD HAVE ALL THE WOMEN I WANT

If I could have all the women I want—WOW!
WOW! You know what I mean by having, don't you?
Let me explain. I mean do what I want with them.
Ask, they would do.
Call, and they would come fulfill my every desire,
When I want, where I want, what I want, and how I want.
WOW! That would be a great day.
I would have a Monday, Tuesday, Wednesday, Thursday, Friday, and Saturday woman. I'd take a break on Sunday to thank God for all the women during the week. Then I would give them all a chance to worship me. You know every man's fantasy is to be worshipped. They could cook my food, clean my house, wash my clothes, and give me a bath. Please don't forget to bathe me. Now, let me see. This is so exciting. What else could I do?
Well, I'll probably have to do a few things for them.
What's wrong with God anyway? What's up with

this monogamy? You can only be married to one woman. Why? He must have forgotten Solomon had it made, 700 wives, 300 concubines. All for his pleasure. That's living, you see. Solomon... wait a minute...all those women did turn his heart away from God...the kingdom was divided...and he wasted his wisdom on the wrong thing. Forget Solomon. Let's look at somebody else.

David! Now King David had it made for sure. He had his own wives, Michal, Abigail, and a few other women. Don't forget about beautiful Bathsheba. Bathsheba was...wait...maybe we should forget about Bathsheba. David killed Uriah...his children hated each other...his own son tried to kill him... and he was punished by God. Forget David!

I know—Abraham. Abraham, the father of faith, had Sarah, and then he had Hagar with his wife's permission. Now that was living. Abraham was the man...or was he? Sarah got jealous of Hagar... Ismael was born and he became an enemy to God's people...and Abraham's house never knew peace.

There has to be somebody who had fun with more than one woman. How about Samson? Yep, Samson was a player. Strong, handsome, and he loved women. He could have any woman he wanted, and you knew men wanted Delilah. Delilah wanted Samson...or did she? She cut his hair...he was blinded...tied to a gristmill...and humiliated.

I might need to give this some more thought. You ever thought about shopping with seven women, arguing with seven women, listening to seven women, and trying to understand their feelings? How about providing for them, remembering birthdays, special moments, anniversaries, special colors, likes, dislikes, moods—let me out of here. God, I think I'll do it your way!

IN SEARCH OF ME

Who am I? Why am I?
What, when, and where am I?
Sometimes I feel that the me I've become
is not who I was meant to be,
so I run looking, searching everywhere for *me*.
There are actions I've taken and roads I've traveled
down that have left me in bondage and yearning to
be free. So in my search, I've stopped several times,
wasting time in places, spending time with people,
and working on purposes that were not really a part
of who I am. I just got stuck because I was oblivi-
ous. The present security of that life mesmerized
me like a neon light on Broadway shouting, "This
may not be your real destiny, but it's a good place to
make something out of your life." I embraced the
potential and dreamed of all the good things that
would happen to me—but they didn't happen.
That right woman turned out to be the wrong
woman. The drugs and alcohol I consumed never
helped me find my place. It didn't matter how much
I drank, smoked, snorted, shot up, or popped. I
was never completely satisfied, even after a good

high or a good time or a good night of fun. I still couldn't find me. So I kept searching.

Searching. Still excited, making plans to go on, believing I still had enough desire and joy for living to help me shake off the ghost of my past. I dressed up again, covering the scars. Now armed with a more tattered, battered, and beaten up life, I knew I could make better decisions that would surely help me find me.

Then it started. A silent cycle of frustrated days, when my dreams were drowned by the constant sabotage of my own inability to stay happy and remain stable when I knew it should be better. This led to depression, moments of blaming (look what everybody has done to me), moments of pity (look what I'm going through), and moments of anger. (Stay out of my way. I don't trust you.) When I was sober, I would crash into the reality that I still needed something to complete my search for me.

Someone said, "How about God?" "God," I said. "I've played with God. I've laughed at God. I don't think God can help me." But I was so desperate, I tried Him. Immediately, I knew who I was. I knew why I was. I even knew when, where and what I was. I found me in God. All of me! Not a piece of me. Complete! Whole! Sane!

GRAND POP

Fried fish, baseball games,
His feet propped up on a stool.
That's what I remember about Grand Pop.
Fourth of July, the family barbeque,
And riding in the back of his car to get ice cream.
That's what I remember about Grand Pop.
Needing a toothpick and sucking his teeth,
Waiting until he got his food before we could eat.
That's what I remember about Grand Pop.
He would eat and fall asleep watching the TV,
We got up to change the channel but somehow
he'd see.
That's what I remember about Grand Pop.
Listening to the baseball game on the radio and
on T.V.,
Us kids would marvel that he could still do this
and sleep.
That's what I remember about Grand Pop.
Days of dialysis, riding in a chair,
But still seeing the fire in his stare.
He was growing weaker.
That's what I remember about Grand Pop.

Hearing him talk about Jesus as his Savior at last,
It made me cry when he said "I'm saved," and then
one day he passed.
That's what I remember about Grand Pop.

WHERE IS MY DADDY?

It takes more than a night between the sheets to become a man.

It takes more than hanging out with your friends
And just coming around, stopping around, being around every now and then.

You've been given a precious gift from God to hold in your arms.

Don't you know a child cannot be strong?

When the world is rough, and the streets are tough,

How can they go on?

Where is my daddy? Why didn't he come home?

Didn't he hear my cry? Why did he leave me alone?

Where is my daddy? He's supposed to be there,
And yet he acts like he don't care.

Daddy, don't you see what you're doing when you walk out on me?

It takes more than a gift to ease my mind.

Your money is fine, but what I need is more of your time.

It takes more than promises you don't keep.

What I need is a hand I can hold
As I grow old to keep my heart from growing cold.
Where is my daddy? Daddy, I need you here with me
To pick me up when I skin my knee,
To hold me in your arms so tight, to rock me to sleep at night.
All I get are empty words,
You say you'll call but nothing have I heard.
So many times I've been waiting on you. "Don't you love me?"

YO MAN, HOLLA AT YOUR BOY!

Yo man, holla at your boy!
I need someone to look out for me, too.
Look out for me and I'll look out for you.
I know I'm not supposed to show it,
And you're not supposed to know it.
We ain't supposed to go there,
But I need someone I can talk to about my stuff.
Yo man, holla at your boy!
No, I ain't funny,
But I need a friend that won't be phony,
Who I can be around
And not have to be cool.
And even when I act a fool
By breaking the man rules,
Which say don't act like you need somebody,
But I need someone I can talk to about my stuff.
Yo man, holla at your boy!
I need a friend that won't put me down,
Who will give advice that is sound.
A true friend to the end
Who will even be there when things are going
wrong,

When I mess up will come at me real strong.

Who will find me and say, "Yo man, what's up?"

I need a brotha, a homeboy, a partner, a roadie, a secret-keeper, not afraid to be a weeper. When I hurt, you hurt. When I'm cool, you're cool, and we cool. A call anytime and tell me what's on your mind kinda friend. An "I'm gonna tell you when you're crazy" and a get on you when you're lazy kinda friend.

I need a Bible reader, prayer leader, church going, holiness showing, God loving, Christian brother who is a worshiper and praiser and knows that Jesus is his Savior. A guy not afraid to cry, shout, sing, or jump when the service is pumped, but strong, not a wimpy chump. Someone who can get a prayer through, and in times of trouble knows just what to do. Look out for me and I'll look out for you.

Yo man, holla at your boy! All I'm saying is you don't have to hurt alone.

You've got a friend, open up and let me in.

I won't let you down.

I love you, man.

FAILURE

Failure.

Who? Not me.

I don't...I can't...you must be kidding.

I'm not the kind of guy who fails; I'm the one who does the winning.

At least that's what I show everybody, at least that's what I sell.

The real truth I dare not admit; the real truth I really don't want to tell.

Men don't handle failure well.

We get depressed. Yeah, men get depressed, but we dress it up and cover it up.

We're good at not letting anyone get close.

We fear you may see the tracks of our tears.

We never cry out loud. We make sure we cry when no one can hear.

We drink, we drug, in order to self medicate.

We holler and scream, and it seems we have a very short fuse to what we can take.

Men don't handle failure well.

I'M ADDICTED

Strong...................... Most days, weak.
Standing tall .... But frequently I fall.
I could have a future .. I have a dark past.
I'm addicted.
Dependable................ I'm also deceitful.
Looking for a job .... But I'll steal if I have to.
Honest...................... Sometimes I'm an awful liar.
I'm addicted.
Controlling nothing, messing up everything,
Driven by urges that some days make me forget what I should be doing.
Living for the next fix, stepping on whoever
I can't help it, because I'm addicted.
Pain, hurt, guilt, and shame.
Everyone I have used is now hip to my game.
I say I will change, But I get worse.
Can someone please help me with my addiction?
"He whom the Son sets free is free indeed."
"There is nothing too hard for God."
When you're weak, He is strong.
Maybe I should be addicted to Jesus.

LOVE SONGS, TV, AND MOVIES

I'm all alone, inside my fears with only darkness for a friend.
I can't pretend now; I am hurting inside.
My smiling face and empty phrase is only good for show and tell,
But with all this pain, to myself I can't lie.
My whole world is falling down around me because I heard you're getting married.
I've seen this plot at least a thousand times, but the reality is blowing my mind.
This should only happen in love songs, on TV, or in the movies,
And I can't believe that it's happening to me.
As a matter of fact, this only happens in love songs, or TV, or in the movies.
Why did it have to happen to me?
A rain drop hits my window pane. Another lonely night has come.
I can't pretend; now I'm hurting inside.
Sitting here on the bed thinking deeply about us,
I can't believe that you are out of my life.
I always thought that I wanted to be free

Until I heard you were getting married.
I should have treated you better the time we were together.
And now you're over me, but I'm not over you.
I've seen the plot at least a thousand times, but the reality is blowing my mind.
This should only happen in love songs, on TV, or in the movies,
And I can't believe that it is happening to me.
As a matter of fact, this only happens in love songs, on TV, or in the movies.
I'm losing you. I'm losing you ...

THE MASK

Did you know when you see me you are not seeing me because I wear a mask?

I wear it so you can see what you need to see.

Although what you see is not really me: you are looking at my mask.

I need the mask because it's hard sometimes, being a man.

Not in the sexual sense, but in the too many roles and responsibilities sense.

It sometimes intimidates me to try to be the perfect man in all situations

When I know my imperfections quite well.

But with my mask, I can be just like all the other men,

Talking trash and if you confront me, ready to smash.

I can even be bold and brash,

And don't even try to give me no sass.

And if I am called on, I can usually fake any task all because I wear my mask.

I have a daddy mask that says this family is safe.

I've got a husband mask that says, don't worry I've got this.

What you can't, I can take.

I've got a job mask. I am more intelligent than all the rest.

I've got an "I can handle it" mask—go ahead, put me to the test.

And last but not least, "I don't have to explain or communicate" mask because I am a man.

You see, I hold it in when I should let it out.

I get angry when all I need is a good pout,

But that is not manly.

I fight when it is time to share.

I have secret fears eating at my soul with so many burdens that I never really feel whole.

And so I wear the mask.

The man mask, the one that makes me qualified.

The one that allows me to keep going straight ahead, even when I want to turn aside.

Do you want to see the real me? Do you want to know what's behind the mask?

Hurting makes me hurt.

Pain is still pain.

Emotional insecurity also affects me.

I cry. That's right, cry!

But only on the inside.
That mask is so good that some days I have even got myself fooled.
I probably need to take it off.

WHY MEN LOOK

I need to put this to rest. I need to put this problem to bed.

Many times we've been misunderstood and many wrong things have been said

About why men look at other women.

I'm not trying to defend it because God knows it's wrong.

I'm just trying to explain it so any man hooked will understand the problem with stolen looks.

You remember when Christ said when you look, you lust. It's not just your eyes; your heart's been touched.

Don't front, don't lie. I've heard all the alibis.

It affects every man because it starts inside. Inside, that's right,

But let me back up before I give you real understanding about this stuff.

It's not because we aren't satisfied with our wives and ready to lay them aside.

It's not because we are fantasizing about being intimate, not all the time.

It's not because we're on the hunt, not all the time.

A lot of these situations can be part of the maze, But they're still not the only reasons that we continue to gaze.

Here it goes. It's not earth shattering, but it's true—men look because *we want to*.

There, I said it. It's not an out of control impulse, not some compelling internal wiring by God.

We like looking. There's something natural and manly about looking.

But in reality, there is no mystery. It's been the same all through history. Men like to look.

Part II

GOD
"God...always guiding, always keeping,
always loving, always there."

I SEE GOD

There's a bright moon shining over the Caribbean Sea. The wind is smoothly sailing through the trees causing a rhythmic dance that hypnotizes anyone who dares to get caught in the view. It's a beautiful sight on a beautiful night, but, "I see God."

The snowcapped glacier is glistening in the early morning sun. The clear voice of a bird can be heard singing gratefully because the storm is done. The mountain peaks create a panoramic backdrop that leaves you breathless. Each breath of mountain air sends a cold chill that tingles the body when swallowed. Its beauty is beyond compare, but even as I stare, "I see God."

There's a lawnmower humming in the distance, and an ice cream truck melodically rolls by. Kids run through the streets, and the flowers become temporary resting places for the bees. It's summertime, the time of year that can blow your mind. Baseball games, hot dogs, barbeque pits, iced tea, lemonade, vacations, and trips. When I finally settle on my back steps, the dust dropping a velvet cape for nature's nighttime rest, I'm glad I'm here to play my part, but in my heart, "I see God."

I FOUND IT

I knew it!
I've always known it!
I told you!
I knew it must exist.
I knew it had to exist
Or you and I and so many others would not have
been looking for it.
I went looking for it in all the wrong places.
I faked it, pretended, and even lied.
I didn't want anyone to know that I didn't have it,
but I didn't.
I don't have to pretend anymore because I found
it!
I got it!
It's mine!
I found a better life in Christ!

WATCH OUT FOR A LITTLE

(Wrestling With My Conscience)
Oooh, that lady sure was fine
As she walked by strutting, strolling, shaking her behind.
Don't get mad at me because I looked; God made me that way.
What's wrong with a little look, anyway?
Blessed Assurance, Jesus Is Mine!
You think because we are in church, you have a strong case.
Man, I looked at that woman, turned back still singing, and never even lost my place.
I've got it like that, you know. I'm all in once the worship starts.
What's that you say, how can I have God and lust in my heart?
That's a good question. I was just looking, not lust-ing. I told you before.
I've got everything under control, and I know I'm saved for sure.
I've only fallen a few times, and that's because I wasn't focused and praying.

But now I've got it together—you heard all those Bible verses I've been saying.

Blessed Assurance, Jesus Is Mine!

I know! I know! I'm looking again!

All right, all right! I was lusting, but just a little. Give me a break.

At least I keep it real and I'm not like most of these fakes. *(It was just a little.)*

What's that you say, a little is all it takes?

A little what? A little leaven leavens the whole lump.

A little deceit can put your whole walk in the dump.

A little anger made Cain kill Abel.

A little fear made Peter unstable.

A little doubt made Jesus' hometown lose their blessing,

And a little lust had David confessing.

Now I'm your conscience,

And I'm not saying you did anything wrong.

But watch out—a little can be dangerous.

I'm just sounding the alarm.

All right, conscience, you want me to be careful! That's cool!

Thank you for helping me turn things around.

Oooh, here she comes again,
But this time I think I'll keep my head down.

I SHOULD BE SLEEPING

Tic Toc, Tic Toc, it's twelve, one, two o'clock.
My mind says sleep, my heart overrides,
And my physical body is hurt and tired.
My fits and my failures, my rights and my wrongs
Are dancing through my mind like a never-ending
song.
It's late, I'm awake, and I should be sleeping.
Tic Toc, Tic Toc, it's one, two, three o'clock.
I wish I may, I wish I might,
I wish I had put up a stronger fight.
I wrestled and lost but could have held out.
I don't know why it's so clear now,
But when I'm in confrontation, I doubt.
Give in, fall, and sin again.
Now I find myself in this condition.
It's late, I'm awake, and I should be sleeping.
Tic Toc, Tic Toc, it's eight o'clock.
The last thing I remember was praying.
Oh, God, make this long night stop.
I must trust in you with all you can do.
I've been through a lot, but at least I made it
through.

I'm not perfect, I mess up, I don't have all I need.
But I've got to stop making this fuss, especially when it's time to sleep.
With the clock steadily ticking away my time,
While I let stuff that hasn't happened or can't be changed clutter up my mind.
Thank you, Lord. I'm going to sleep now.
Tic Toc, Tic Toc,
And for the next few hours, I slept like a rock.

MERCY (Psalms 100:5)

Nothing else could have made a difference;
Nothing else could have made me free.
No one else knew what I did.
No one but you knew all of me.
But you gave me mercy.
For a brief moment my heart turned dark,
And I did what I said I'd never do again.
Yet in spite of my inconsistencies,
You looked past my faults and called me friend.
And you gave me mercy.
I held my breath as I walked into the service.
I was acting as normal as I could.
There was shame in my heart and sorrow on my mind.
Everyone had to know what I did; I was just no good.
But you gave me mercy.
I needed help, I felt so bad,
All my sins had been discovered.
I looked up and cried, "Lord, forgive me!"
Then it came, new mercy, and I was fully covered,
When you gave me mercy.

It ran from my heart, down my arms to my hands.
I felt so light-footed that I began to dance.
I got bolder with each praise; I was swimming in forgiveness.
I opened up completely, free from the stress.
When you gave me mercy.

IT'S YOU

What is this strength? What is this joy that swallows me up inside?
I am growing stronger every day since the old man has died.
What makes me feel like things are going right, even when they look wrong?
What makes me know that I can face anything, and still be strong?
It is real now, and what I feel now, I will tell you the reason why.
Jesus, it is you; you are my morning star.
Jesus, it's you; your love's shining in my heart.
Jesus, it is you.

I NEED A PLACE TO REST

Rest is hard to find in this unstable world
Constantly bombarding my mind with placebos
that stop the pain,
But only for a little while.
These substitutes can sometimes even make me
smile,
All the time perpetrating
That what they are doing is for my best.
But in the end I still need rest.

I TURN IT OVER TO YOU

There it is again, breaking through the roar, through office noise, street sounds, and a multitude of voices.

I hear it as clear as a bell, refusing to be dismissed, pushing it way to the top of my list.

There, hear it? It's my Conscience, ready to lecture, debate, berate, and belittle.

Trying with a gangster-like fashion to grip the reigns of my mind in a relentless stampeding attack.

It is trying to help me resolve the riddle of my going astray; it won't go away, constantly reminding me of my battle.

You probably experienced it, one moment grounded, settled, moving triumphantly in the divine direction, not yielding to temptation.

Sickness or struggle, handling all obstacles as easily as Superman bending steel with his bare hands.

Look, there in the church! What is it? Worshiping, serving, and leading, it's a vision. It's an angel? No, it's Super-Christian! Able to lift tall problems with a single prayer.

Super-Christian—creases in his pants, shine on his shoes. Doesn't drink, smoke, or use.

Sometimes disguised, yes, disguised. This changing back and forth from holy to heathen is hard to take. Sometimes I feel like all of this is just a disguise, or at best, a discontented lie.

From a dusty cavern jail cell, I hear the Apostle Paul telling me clearly how to think. "Only on things that are true."

How to fight, "casting down imaginations," that sometimes haunt,

And how to stand, "having done all to stand, keep standing."

But when the world starts calling and my flesh starts falling, what am I to do?

Suddenly, I lay my head down in exhaustion. With my strength running out, I pray.

Then, I turn it over to you, a friend, a Father, a helper, someone who cares.

As I relax through the night, you fight the battle, gently restoring, building up my heart, and drying my tears. I turn it over to you, and somehow you fix it.

When I awake, it starts all over again. I start to lose, then turn it over to you and win.

LESS OF ME

Less of me is what I need,
More of you if I'm to be free.
I say I'm grown but sometimes I act like a child.
Pouting, angry, losing control,
Making bad decisions that have nothing to do with my faith in God,
My actions testifying that there are still a few demons in my soul, alive and well
Bringing me captive to the reality that without you I would lose more battles and be living in hell. Now, I can't even count the times that I thought about, thought about! Oh, no! Dwelt on the wrong thing so long that it felt like it was the right thing, even the thing that I was missing, not only missing but needing, like a junkie searching for a familiar hit to ease the jones for just a little while. You know, like the feeling you got the first time you heard E.T. phone home or the cool and cruel Macaulay Culkin in Home Alone, cruising, abusing, and bruising the bad guys. You know it's wrong but it's all in fun, right? That's the way it seems. But if you

don't stay in control of your actions, I have learned that kind of fun can kill you.

Less of me is what I need,

More of you if I'm ever going to be free.

No matter how spiritual I get, when I take over it is anything goes. I nod off with no restraints.

Somebody wake me up so I can start doing what I'm saying, and being instead of playing. It all becomes so surreal, no longer driven nor guided by faith but how I feel,

The rush of emotions, and the high of the moment make good alibis. But it seems at last, I've got to crash and pay the piper for the dance. Here it comes, that all too eerie, scary process called repentance.

A burning conscience and a soul that's trying to become whole. Thanking God that he is the one who is keeping score, not me, not my enemy, and not even the self-righteous saints who want to make you think they have never been tempted.

And if they ever were, they know they would never act like you.

Victory is mine; victory is mine.

Most of the time I can say that, just not today.

I'm too weak, too frustrated, and if you want to

know the truth, it's just the grace of God that I've never given up when I choose the things I choose. *Less of me* is what I need,
More of you if I'm ever really going to be free.
I'm the happiest when I'm in your will,
It's tough and it's rough, and most days I want to shout *enough*!
But by the time I get ready to give up, I remember *you're there with more.*

Part III

US
"There is no me, there is no you, if there is no us."

I'LL LOVE YOU BACK

Honey, I'm hurting, and I don't know what else to say.
I've hinted, begged, cried, and you still act the same way.
If you love me, I'll love you back any way you want.
Just don't let the fire in our marriage burn out because of the things you don't do.
Honey, I'm hurting because after all this time, you don't understand my needs.
You say I'm a good man, you say I'm the one.
However, I seldom get pleased.
I'm sorry that physical love means so much,
But even God said we shouldn't deprive one another.
Honey, I'm hurting, now I'm not going astray.
I love you and God too much to act that way.
But there are limits to what a man can stand.
Please take time and let's fix this. I'll do all I can.
Our marriage is precious, but I can't go on hurting.
Just meet me halfway, we can make it. I'm certain.

Honey, I'm hurting, and although I love you still,
I'm finding my mind wandering. There's a weakening of my will.
I know you depend on my relationship with God to keep us secure.
I depend on it, too. That's why I'm trying harder and giving more.
If you want to know what's really going on,
What could turn our marriage to an oasis and keep it strong,
Then you need to know, honey, I'm hurting, I really am.

THE PERFECT NIGHT

Dinner,
A movie,
And making love,
The perfect night.
Cutting grass,
Shopping all day,
Helping to put the food away,
And making love,
The perfect night.
Having friends over to entertain,
Playing games and having fun,
Tired but glad everything's done,
And making love,
The perfect night.
Playing basketball, watching the game,
You gone all day shopping and playing,
Having a fight, make up that night,
And making love,
The perfect night.
Going to worship,
Had a good time,
And making love,
The perfect night.

WHAT IS IT?

What is it that makes me want to be near you, hear you, feel you, hold you, touch you, speak to you, call and cry out your name? What is it? Is it your eyes? I've seen hundreds of eyes, no, hundreds of thousands of pairs of eyes. I've seen lips and hips, some thick, some thin, thighs of all sizes, but they're not yours.

What is it? Is it your smile? Your smile may not light up every room, but it lights up every room that I'm in. When I'm near you, I'm secure. When we're apart, I realize how much time I wasted not appreciating you. When we we're together, all I can think of is more, more, I need more of you. More of your laughter, your frowns, and even more of the silent moments when you're in deep thought but you're still around.

What is it? I really tried to figure it out. Especially when we're mad, you get mad at me, or I get mad at you, I just want to take flight and find another you. Oh, what things the new you and me will do! But my thoughts stop soaring and I come back to reality. My problem is that when it's over, I will still only want you.

What a dilemma. What a sweet up, down, mind-boggling dilemma. What is it? To just call it love only touches the surface. To call it desire cheapens the reality of my longings. I'm tired and bewildered from trying to figure it out. I know what I'll do. Whatever it is, I've got it. I think I'll just enjoy it.

I'M TIRED

Father, husband, friend, and lover.
Keeper, provider, and spiritual cover.
I'm tired.
Plumber, lawn service, shopper, and chef.
Bill payer, thing fixer, and clean up the mess.
I'm tired.
Be soft and warm, cuddly and cute,
Be strong and able and know how to soothe.
I'm tired.
Please listen, don't sleep. I just need you to hear.
Don't talk to me now, but please calm my fear.
I'm tired.
Don't cry, don't be fearful and handle all the struggles.
Be like all other good men; don't cause trouble.
I'm tired.
Dad, can you? Honey, will you? Mister, you better!
I know I make this man thing look light as a feather.
But sometimes I'm just tired.

SURE WISH I KNEW WHAT YOU WERE THINKING

Sure wish I knew what you were thinking.
It's hard to guess all the time.
I'm trying to act like I know without blinking,
But I'm gonna blow a fuse and lose my mind.
When I think you're happy, you say, "I feel like crying."
When something happens, I want to help,
But you say, "Leave me alone, I'm fine."
Sure wish I knew what you were thinking.
If I buy a gift as a surprise, you say, "You shouldn't have."
If I don't buy a gift after you tell me not to, you say,
"If you loved me, you would have."
If I say fried chicken, you say Chinese.
If I say, "Cook dinner," you say, "You're hard to please."
If I plan a surprise to be romantic, you say,
"You should have told me. I've got nothing to wear."

If I tell you to choose where you want to go, you say,
"Surprise me! I need romance. Don't you care?"
Sure wish I knew what you were thinking.
When I say, "I want you to go with me," you say,
"You should have checked the schedule."
When I say I'm going alone, you say,
"Why don't you want me to go with you?"
When I say I'm sorry, you say,
"You don't really mean it."
When I don't say I'm sorry, you say,
"You're just mean!"
I guess I'll never know what you're thinking,
But it sure would help.

I LIKE EVERYTHING ABOUT YOU

I like you mad,
I like you glad,
I like to hold you when you're sad.
I like you happy,
I like you bothered,
I like you through our good times and bad.
I like everything about you.
I like your smell,
I like your touch,
I like the little wrinkles in your nose when you rush.
I like the way you comb your hair,
I like the deepness of your care,
I like the way I get lost in your smile.
I like everything about you.

MARRIAGE

Marriage.
A tuxedo, a gown, flowers, and a limousine.
A girl in love with a boy who has captured the girl of his dreams.
A church, a preacher, a ceremony, and rice.
Pictures, a kiss, a meal, and off they go to paradise.
They settle in, adjustments, arguments, and anger discovered.
Two people evolving, living together, who never really knew each other.
I thought you were nice, I thought you were understanding,
I thought our relationship was special. But I'm coming down, and it's not a happy landing.
The kids, the bills, the different perspective heightens the confusion.
This marriage thing is work; the happily ever after was just an illusion.
The hurts, the failures, the injustices mount up.
An explosion—BANG—a hug. The pattern of ups and downs makes our emotions erupt.

Sometimes comfortable, committed, and even content with our choice.

Those days of running and giving up seem few, and the thoughts of divorce are distant.

The sacrifices, struggles, and pulling together take their toll,

But you know deep in your heart that without each other, you're not whole.

A tuxedo, a gown, flowers, and a limousine.

It's your children's turn now to walk the aisles, and you are proud.

A quick glance at each other says it seems impossible, but we made it somehow.

THE AFFAIR

It's wrong and it's right; it's right and it's wrong.

It's weak in its explanation, but oh, so physically strong,

At least for a while; okay, it's wrong, wrong, wrong.

I should have stayed home, but let me alone.

Let me explain. I'm sorting through this as fast as I can.

I'm trying to recall what led to the first weekend and my involvement in

The Affair

Sure, we had love at home, once hot, sweet, and nice.

It got dull and routine with glances of ice.

Comments, the work, bills, and kids got in the way.

No time for love; responsibility was the call of the day.

Did you do this or didn't I tell you to do that? So much pressure that the only way to survive is

You do yours, and I'll do mine.

Stay out of each other's way, and we can live together just fine.

We're saved and we're married; Hallelujah, we're blessed.

But we sure made this relationship

A Mess

Now we're going through the motions

With pains and hurt deeper than four oceans.

Praying and staying,

Putting all our faith in God. Pretending and extending.

Once in a while things seem to be on the mend then you realize you're living with a stranger who at one time was your best friend.

Settled in, going along, thinking, *hey, this is just the way it is.*

Good days, bad days, ain't no use complaining. It must be something I did.

Now your needs and her needs get lost in the shuffle, and now it seems that every day you're just hoping not to tussle.

All you want is a place of rest, and sure enough, here it comes.

Hope you're ready for the

The Test

"Hey," she says. "You got the time?"

"Sure." You smile. "It's just a little after nine."

And all the while you're thinking she sure is fine.

Whoa! A body that can blow your mind.

"Thank-you," she says. You turn and she's still looking.

The vibes are running hot and your blood starts to cooking.

I haven't felt like this in a long time. Finally a woman who talks sweet and kind.

"You're welcome!" you holler back in your sexiest voice.

See you around! Bingo! Jackpot! Look what I just found.

The stage is set. You see her again and again, flirting, laughing, talking.

She becomes your new best friend.

Respect and manners, your manhood drives her crazy.

She's soft and lovely, and when you're around her, everything gets hazy.

Now the talks are therapeutic and the attraction grows stronger.

The time together gets longer and longer.

She's the only one who understands you, the only one who really cares.

She's there for you and bears with you. Why can't my wife be like that?

The emotional becomes physical, the physical becomes normal, until you look up one day and you're all in.

Lying, scheming, hiding, believing that this somehow is going to

Turn Out

The music is playing; the mood is right.

We're indulging in our love and are going to have a good life.

But are we? There are things we can't do.

There are fences and hurdles we can't climb.

We can never be seen affectionate in the daylight.

Who wants to live in a midnight life?

The hugs and the kisses aren't enough.

The promises turn into lies; even this relationship is losing trust.

Something must give; something must break.

There's got to be more; this is turning into heartbreak.

We're only making a down payment on future pain.

The "hellos" and "I will call you" is now just a game.

The reality is that if it's love, you can't have it. You're taking heartache you didn't need.

If it's not love and just a habit, you gave a piece of your life you can never get back.

Now there's more baggage in your heart that needs to be

Unpacked

It's wrong and it's right; it's right and it's wrong.

It's weak in its explanation, but oh, so physically strong,

At least for a while; okay, it's wrong, wrong, wrong.

I should have stayed home, but let me alone.

Let me explain. I'm sorting through this as fast as I can.

I'm trying to recall what led to the first weekend and my involvement in

The Affair

I need to get out, I need to look up, and it's getting rough.

I'm drowning and I don't know whom to trust.

I could lose my family and my future, be financially stripped of my reputation.

Suddenly it hits me, the realization. I need to
repent. I hate it.

I hope it's not too late. I hope I didn't hurt too
many people.

Lord, just help, rescue me from

The Affair

"I'M CRAZY ABOUT YOU"

I can't think.
I can't sleep,
I can't eat.
My mind is consumed with continuous thoughts
of your
>   Smile
>   Your face
And your voice.
I think I'm crazy about you.
Other things make me laugh.
Other things make me smile,
Other things occupy my time.
But even when I'm doing them, I'm thinking of
your
>   Smile
>   Your face
>   And your voice.
I think I'm crazy about you.
Will you hurt me? Will you heal me?
When I taste your love, will it thrill me?
Take away the void and fill me, or will it eventually
kill me?

I don't know why I'm willing to take the chance,
But this feeling is so real.

I want to swirl you around in my arms and float to the highest point of heaven where we can be alone, you and me dancing above the mundane, every day circumstances that cheat and rob us of the romance that triggers feelings like these, that brings us back down to earth and takes strong, loving, capable men like me and turns us into selfish little boys or prideful, self-protecting men who are incapable of really riding the joy and bliss of moments like these.

I want to shout it to the world; I want everyone to know.

It's pounding inside and it excites me so.

But alas, because I'm a man, these kinds of feelings I can't show!

You know I love you baby, but a man has got to be cool, subdued, and running things. That's the rules. So instead of telling you constantly how much I love you, I don't tell you at all and expect you to continue to fall deeply in love with me even though the only real affection

I show is in the bedroom. And that isn't right, only being in love at night. I'm trying to tell you that ain't real. This is how I really feel, and if you could only remember these words when I'm less affectionate than I should be, if you would look past my actions into my soul. Even though I don't say it often and we drift apart, I want you to know.

I can't think.

I can't sleep.

I can't eat.

My mind is consumed with continuous thoughts of

Your smile

Your face

And your voice.

I *know* I'm crazy about you.

Help!

Love me!

Please!

Save this crazy man.

I FOUND YOU

Sometimes in life, roads are changed and feelings die.

But if we are strong, we'll find love and we'll survive.

I found you waiting with open arms to make me strong.

I found you.

I found in you a resting place for all my fears.

I found you.

I have just begun to feel the strength of a love that is real.

Dreams I no longer need; I am touching you. New life, I feel

I found you.

You supplied my every need, unlocked my heart, and you hold the key.

I found you.

Undying love in you I found, always around.

I found you.

You picked up the pieces of my broken heart and helped me make it through.

Then I opened up the window and let your love shine in;
Now my heart is shining for only you.
I found you waiting with opened arms to make me strong.
I found you.
I found in you a resting place for all my fears.
You supplied my every need, unlocked my heart, and you hold the key.
Undying love in you I found, always around.
You never let me down.
I found you.

BONUS

Five Irresistible Characteristics That Men Find Attractive In Women

These poems are derived from the comments of hundreds of men who participated in intense workshops on issues that confront them. Most of the crucial issues that men deal with come from their inabilities to form lasting and substantial relationships. From this work, I have been able to construct the following five characteristics that men find attractive. They are listed in the order of importance based on my research:

💜 Men love women who take care of themselves and

spend time making themselves attractive. I found that men like women who are comfortable with their femininity and are well-groomed for every situation.

💜 Men love women who can be sarcastic without being mean. Men love a good sense of humor, but also a woman who can joust during a conversation with just enough edge on her comments to let you know she can be playful and intelligent.

💜 Men love women who are passive-aggressive in the bedroom. Intimacy is very important to a man. In fact, it is high on his list of priorities. No man likes a prudish woman who cannot lead when need be in the area of sexual intimacy, but they also don't want the woman to be crude and offensive in this area.

💜 Men love women who are supportive and helpful through difficult periods. Most men are devastated when they fail or if they are constantly doing the wrong thing. A woman who is tactful in her support and constructive in her criticism is very attractive.

♥ Men love women who can be independent and show that they still need their man. This is a definite turn-on to any man because of the inherent need to feel like the protector and problem-solver.

WHAT GOD IS SAYING TO ME

(Your Thoughts & Reflections)

_____

_____

_____

_____

_____

_____

_____

_____

_____

_____

_____

_____

_____

_____

_____
_____
_____
_____
_____
_____
_____
_____
_____
_____
_____
_____
_____
_____
_____
_____
_____
_____
_____
_____
_____
_____
_____
_____
_____

WHAT GOD IS SAYING TO ME

(Your Thoughts & Reflections)

_____

_____

_____

_____

_____

_____

_____

_____

_____

_____

_____

_____

_____

_____

_____

_____

_____

_____

_____

_____

_____

_____

_____

_____

_____

_____

_____

_____

_____

_____

_____

_____

_____

_____

_____

_____

_____
_____
_____
_____
_____
_____
_____
_____
_____
_____
_____
_____
_____
_____
_____
_____
_____
_____
_____
_____
_____
_____
_____
_____
_____
_____